CRACOW
A City of Kings

CRACOW
A City of Kings

 Wydawnictwo PARMA® PRESS

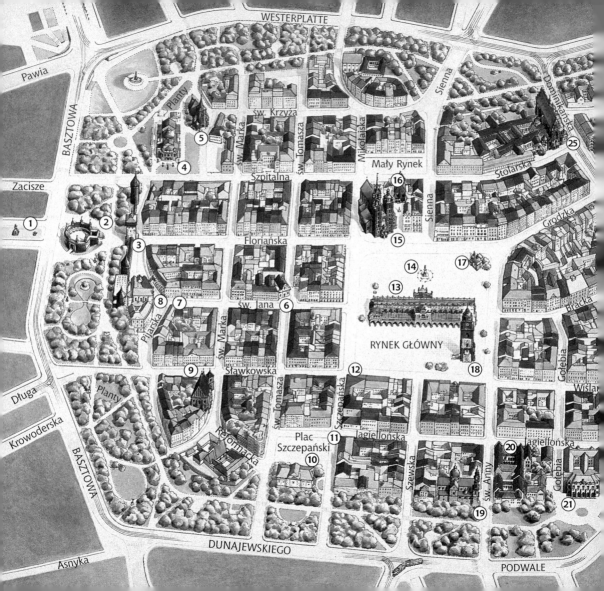

CRACOW

1. Matejko Square
2. The Barbican
3. The Florian Gate
4. The Słowacki Theatre
5. The Church of the Holy Cross
6. St. John's Church
7. The Czartoryski Museum
8. The Piarite Church
9. St. Mark's Church
10. The Palace of Art
11. The Old Theatre
12. The Krzysztofory Palace
13. The Cloth Hall
14. The Adam Mickiewicz Monument
15. St. Mary's Church
16. St. Barbara's Church
17. St. Adalbert's Church
18. The Town Hall Tower
19. St. Anne's Church
20. Collegium Maius
21. Collegium Novum
22. The Bishop's Palace
23. The Franciscan Church
24. The Archaeological Museum
25. The Dominican Church
26. The Bernardine Church
27. The Church of St. Peter and St. Paul
28. Collegium Iuridicum
29. St. Andrew's Church
30. St. Martin's Church
31. St. Giles's Church
32. The Tadeusz Kościuszko Monument
33. The Royal Cathedral
34. The Royal Castle
35. The Archaeological Reserve
36. The Sandomierska Tower
37. The Złodziejska Tower
38. The Dragon Cave

CRACOW

At the foot of the Carpathians, by the Vistula, lies a city which occupies a special place in the heart of every Pole. This is Kraków, a place whose significance is closely linked with history, and not merely its own, but that of the whole Polish nation. For many years this was the capital city of the country. The heart of Kraków is the Old Town surrounded by the Planty – areas of greenery which appeared where the defensive ramparts removed in the early 19th century had once stood. Fine remnants of these walls are still to be seen in the form of the Barbican (Barbakan) and the Florian Gate. The Planty area is fine for a rest. The Old Town retains the shape conferred upon it in the 12th century, with the arrangement of streets and central location of the Market Square having survived all the periods of reconstruction in the city.

The Main Market Square (Rynek Główny) was for centuries the centre of the religious, economic and administrative life of Kraków. Standing in the middle of it is the Sukiennice (Clothiers' Hall), which was established as early as in the second half of the 12th century. Today, as ever, this is a place of stalls featuring souvenirs and the output of local craftsmen. The rooms on the first floor in turn house a gallery of 19th century Polish painting. The works of Jan Matejko, Piotr Michałowski, Józef Chełmoński, Jacek Malczewski and the Gierymski brothers can be seen there.

The largest building on the Square is the Mariacki (St. Mary's) Church, which is Kraków's principal place of worship. Its beginnings stretch back to the 13th century. The bugle call heard daily on radio at midday is in fact sounded hourly from the Church's higher tower, with each rendition being cut short, in remembrance of the death of a trumpeter long ago from the arrow of one of the invading Tartars. Inside the Church stands the altar carved in the 15th century by Veit Stoss – the largest work of Late Mediaeval woodcarving in Poland.

The Market Square is lined by tenement houses and mansions. The most splendid of these are the Krzysztofory Mansion, the Spis mansion, the Pod Baranami ("Under the Rams") Mansion and the Zbaraski Mansion. There are also many cafes and restaurants. Among them, the Hawełka and Wierzynek restaurants have been in existence for many centuries and have played host to crowned heads, not only of Poland.

Standing in front of St Mary's Church is the Monument to Adam Mickiewicz, another symbol of the city that attracts every visitor. Nearby, the famous flower-sellers ply their trade, while the first days of December witness an extraordinary competition for the most beautiful Kraków nativity scene.

Kraków has also long been a seat of learning. The Jagiellonian University, founded here in the 14th century, has moulded many generations of the intelligentsia. Copernicus was here, and so was Karol Wojtyła, now better known as Pope John Paul II. The Wawel Hill – an escarpment above the Vistula – was the seat of many of Poland's Kings. Its Castle and Cathedral have stood here side by side across the centuries, the former as a Royal residence and the latter as a venue for coronations and a final resting place.

The Castle has been through many transformations. Fires destroyed it, but it was rebuilt. Originally Romanesque in style, it took on a powerful Gothic form from the 14th century onwards. Conversions two centuries later left it with the Renaissance appearance that can still be seen today. The largest ornamentation of the castle apartments are the tapestries brought to Wawel in the 16th century by King Zygmunt August. Part of the fine collection has survived to this day. Next to the Castle is the Cathedral which was for years the most important sanctuary in the Polish lands. From the 14th century times of King Władysław the Short onwards, this was the last resting place of almost all the rulers of Poland. It was also the place where Kings placed votive offerings in the form of the spoils of war won from their defeated enemies. The Cathedral contains the sarcophagi of Kings Władysław Jagiełło (died 1434), Władysław the Short (1333), Kazimierz the Great (1370) and Queen Jadwiga (1399). Placed in the centre is the silver coffin of St. Stanisław. Among a number of surrounding chapels, the finest is that of King Zygmunt the Old.

The crypts contain many more graves of Kings, but those of royal blood are joined by other outstanding Poles. Poets Adam Mickiewicz and Juliusz Słowacki lie here, as do the great military commanders Tadeusz Kościuszko and Marshal Józef Piłsudski. One of the three Cathedral towers known as the Zygmunt Tower holds the Zygmunt Bell cast in the 16th century. This is only sounded at the most important Church festivals and at times of national celebration or commemoration.

Kraków has its own unique feel. For centuries, it has brought together artists and those who shine in every field. This was of crucial importance during the period of Poland's absence from the map of Europe (1795-1918). Kraków was then a refuge, but also a stronghold, of Polish culture and national identity.

While the city's monuments and works of art stood in continuing testimony to history and statehood, the great writers and poets based here ensured its place in the national literature.

Poland is now once again independent, in every sense, but Kraków continues to play a role of this kind, being at once a modern, forward-looking city and a custodian of old achievements and ways. At Corpus Christi, the processions wend their way from the Wawel Castle to the Main Town Square in just the way they must always have done. Within the procession, the attention is drawn to the folk costumes from the region of southern Poland. Then there is the Kraków Lajkonik, whose appearance heralds the so-called "Kraków Days" continuing through June in a festival of culture and art filling the streets beneath the Wawel Hill. The Lajkonik is a knight on a wooden horse attired in a colourful Tartar costume designed by the great artist Stanisław Wyspiański (1869-1907). Its capers recall the victory over the Tartars won by Cracovians in the 13th century. June also sees the International Festival of Short Films, while September brings the National Folk Art Fair and an associated market with a multitude of craft items on sale.

The special charm of Kraków continues to draw artists of all kinds, and there are many theatres and galleries. The city has fostered the creative talents of such diverse figures as composer Krzysztof Penderecki, science-fiction writer Stanisław Lem, artist Tadeusz Kantor and the Nobel Prize-winning poet Wisława Szymborska. All in all, then, Kraków bears fine and still vibrantly-active testimony to its country's history, culture and art. Within its walls there is much of which the Polish nation can be proud, and much to entice the interested visitor.

*The 15th century Dean's House on Kanonicza Street
and, in the background, the majestic outlines of buildings on the Wawel Hill.*

Kanonicza Street. To be found here from the 14th century onwards were canonries, i. e. the homes of the Canons of Kraków. To this day this quiet street retains the climate of Old Kraków, while the unusual mixture of architectural styles confers an exceptionally picturesque character upon it.

An ornamental door-knocker at number 11 Kanonicza Street.

The decorative finishings of the portal and window of a house on Kanonicza Street.

*Painted decoration
on the house built
by Jan Długosz on the corner
of Podzamcze and
Kanonicza Streets.*

Looking down Senacka Street to the Archaeological Museum. There was a prison here in the 19th century.

The Franciscan Church with its complex of monastery buildings.

Opposite the Franciscan Church stands the Bishop's Palace. This likeness of Cardinal Adam Sapieha is to be seen in the courtyard there.

The Franciscan Church: the 13th century walls of the apse of the original place of worship, as seen from All Saints' Square.

The Epitaph of Sebastian Petrycy of Pilsen is an Early-Baroque work in the Franciscan Church.

The Neo-Gothic style high altar in the Franciscan
Church is the work of Edward and Zygmunt Stehlik.
The painting "The Apotheosis of St. Francis"
is by Gerhard Flatz.

The "God the Father" stained-glass window
by Stanisław Wyspiański is to be seen in the Franciscan Church.

All Saints' Square with – in the foreground – Walery Godowski's 1887 Monument to Mikołaj Zyblikiewicz (President of Kraków between 1874 and 1880). Removed in 1954, before being reconstructed in 1985, the Monument marks the spot of the destroyed All Saints' Church.

The Gothic Dominican Church of the Holy Trinity dates back to the 13th-15th centuries and still attracts the faithful in large numbers.

One of the bas-reliefs decorating the interior of the Dominican Church.

The interior of the Dominican Church with its Neo-Gothic fixtures.

The Neo-Classical façade of St. Anne's Church was designed by Tylman of Gameren. The decorative interior from 1695-1703 is in turn the work of Baltazar Fontana.

The Planty surrounding the Old Town comprise a ring of green space set out as the defensive walls were pulled down in the 19th century.

The Neo-Gothic Collegium Novum
building of the Jagiellonian University
is the seat of the University authorities.

The courtyard of the University's Collegium
Maius features Late-Gothic cloisters.
The building has been a museum since 1867.

The character of the courtyard
of the Collegium Maius recalls
the universities of Mediaeval Italy.

Not far from
the Collegium Novum
stands this Monument
to Copernicus which
is the work of Cyprian
Godebski from 1900.

The Seccession-style building of the Society of Friends of the Fine Arts, known as the Palace of Art, is on Szczepański Square. The building boasts large exhibition halls.

Busts of Poland's great artists adorn the building of the Society of Friends of the Fine Arts. Here it is Stanisław Wyspiański who has been immortalized in stone.

Seccession-style stained glass above the entrance to the tenement house on 2 Szczepański Square.

A fragment of the 1903 entrance gate to the Old Theatre on Szczepański Square. It is by Franciszek Mączyński and Tadeusz Stryjeński.

A portrait of Helena Modrzejewska (1840-1909), the most outstanding Polish actress whose links with Kraków reflect roles played in the Old Theatre that now bears her name.

The Prałatówka (Prelate's) tenement house with its Late-Renaissance style attic.

The richly-decorated portal of the Prałatówka tenement house.

The view from the Small Market Square side
of the aisleless 15th century Church
of St. Barbara, as well as St. Mary's Church.

The emblems decorating
the Old Town's "Sign
of the Three Limes"
and "Sign of the Ram"
tenement houses.

A girl sports
the regional dress
of the Kraków area.

The 14th century Gothic-style Church
of the Holy Cross stands on Św. Ducha
(Holy Spirit) Square. Its interior boasts
palm vaulting resting on a single column.

The Neo-Renaissance and Eclectic-style building
of the Juliusz Słowacki Theatre is from the late
19th century. It was modelled on the Paris Opera House.

The Monument on Matejko Square pays homage to King Władysław Jagiełło (reigning 1386-1434), having been erected in 1910 – on the 500th anniversary of his famous victory over the Teutonic Knights at the Battle of Grunwald.

The Barbican is a fragment of the city's mediaeval defences. Built in the Gothic style, it boasts seven characteristic turrets.

This Late-Baroque bas-relief on the Florian Gate presents St. Florian himself.

Floriańska Street, with the Florian Gate in the background. From here the Royal Route runs via the Old Town to the Wawel Hill.

The Hejnał tower of St. Mary's Church has a late-Gothic helm roof terminating in a golden crown. Every hour, on the hour, a bugler sounds the famous "Hejnał" bugle-call to all four corners of the world.

The façade of St. Mary's Church with the great window. The stained glass is to the designs of Józef Mehoffer and Stanisław Wyspiański.

Floriańska Street links the Florian Gate with the Main Market Square. St. Mary's Church is to be seen in the background.

The Main Market Square with the Cloth Hall,
St. Mary's Church and a Kraków hackney carriage.

The Margrabska tenement house,
of which a real decorative feature
is the Rococo-style main doorway.

This Lajkonik from the Premonstratensian
(Norbertine) Convent in Zwierzyniec appears
on the Main Market Square each year in time
for the celebration of Corpus Christi.

The "Sign of the Eagle" house on the Market Square.
The Starmach Gallery operating out of the cellar
of this Renaissance tenement house is one of the best
galleries of contemporary art in Poland.

The Adam Mickiewicz Monument in front
of the Cloth Hall is the work of Teodor Rygier.

It was around the Main Market Square that
the life of the Mediaeval city was centred.
Today too this is a place to meet and to take
in some displays or artistic performances.

"The Enchanted Carriage" was the title of a poem
by Konstanty Ildefons Gałczyński. Today's Kraków
carriages, though perhaps a little less magical,
remain a major tourist attraction of the city.

Little Cracovians.

The unique view of the three towers of the Market Square – the Gothic tower of the Town Hall topped by its Baroque-style helm roof is a relic of the building destroyed in the 19th century, while in the background the towers of St. Mary's Church are to be seen.

A musical ensemble in Kraków dress playing in the Market Square.

A part of the Renaissance-style attic of the Cloth Hall, with its stylized monogram of King Kazimierz the Great. This has now become one of the symbols of Kraków itself.

Situated in the centre of the Main Market Square, the Cloth Hall was once a place of traders' stalls. Its history stretches back to the Middle Ages.

The arcades stretching along the longer walls of the Cloth Hall were built on in 1875.

The Cloth Hall was rebuilt in the Renaissance style after the 1555 fire, as well as being restored in the 19th century by specialists including Jan Matejko. The building holds stalls, cafes and art galleries.

The interior of St. Adalbert's. It is said that the saint gave a sermon here in 997, prior to his departure for Prussia.

The Romanesque-style St. Adalbert's Church whose vaults include an archaeological museum exposing the different cultural layers of the Market Square and providing an exhibition on its history.

The Main Market Square – one of Mediaeval Europe's largest town squares – is dominated by the tower of St. Mary's Church.

Mariacki (St. Mary's) Square,
a charming corner by the south
wall of St. Mary's Church.

The "Sign of the
Africans" House
is on the corner
of St. Mary's Square.
Its bas-relief of two
Africans dates back
to the late
17th century.

Serving as a centrepiece
on St. Mary's Square
is a well with the figure
of a schoolboy which
is a copy of a sculpted
figure on the altar
in the Church.

Just around the back
of the monumental St. Mary's
Church, on St. Mary's Square,
is the Church of St. Barbara
with its characteristic
sculpted Gethsemane.

This 1929 bas-relief on the life of Mary can be seen on the side gate of St. Mary's Church. It is the work of Karol Hukan.

A bronze plaque which Pius Weloński had made to honour the memory of King Jan III Sobieski on the 200th anniversary of his victory at the Battle of Vienna.

The Mediaeval stocks on the wall of the southern portal of St. Mary's church. Sinners were put here on holy days: women for nagging, men for drunkenness and working on holy days, but most of all young people for breaking the sixth commandment.

The modern "Crucifixion" sculpture in one of the recesses of the church's apse. The Town Hall tower is to be seen in the background.

A bas-relief on the old altar of St. Mary's Church which is now to be found in the Museum of the Archdiocese.

*The Late-Gothic high altar, produced by Veit Stoss between 1477 and 1489, presents scenes from the lives
of the Virgin Mary and Christ. Together the bas-reliefs and saintly likenesses form a masterpiece of Late-Gothic art.*

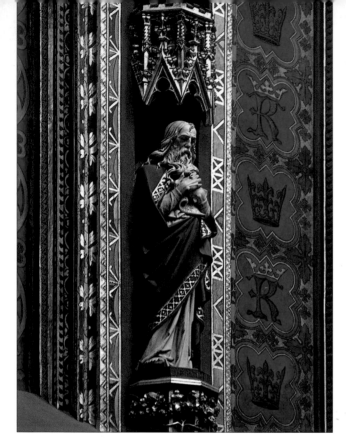

"The Death of the Virgin" – one of the scenes from the life of the Holy Family in the central part of the altar.

The Virgin Mary in the scene presenting "The Descent of the Holy Spirit".

This Gothic figure of the prophet Jeremiah is in the presbytery of St. Mary's Church.

The Tree of Jesse on the altar predella.

In the late evening, the Old Town lures the visitor with its numerous cafes on the Main Market Square.

St. Adalbert's Church and the view down Grodzka Street leading off from the southern corner of the Main Market Square.

Kraków is just as beautiful at night: St. Mary's Church is in the background here.

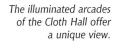

The illuminated arcades of the Cloth Hall offer a unique view.

The bas-relief emblems on a Grodzka Street tenement house.

Grodzka Street is a part of the old Royal Way and one of Kraków's oldest thoroughfares.

The courtyard of the Collegium Iuridicum with its 17th-century arcades. Today the building houses the Jagiellonian Univeristy's Institute of Art History, while the cellar boasts a museum of natural history. Contemporary sculpture by Igor Mitoraj is to be seen in the courtyard.

The Baroque-style ornamentation
to the main portal of the Church
of St. Peter and St. Paul.

Standing in a neat row along
the Church wall are the figures
of the Twelve Apostles sculpted
by Dawid Heel in the years 1715-1722.

Part of the ornate doorway
leading into the Church
of Sts. Peter and Paul.

The Baroque façade of St. Peter and Paul's recalls the Il Gesu Church in Rome. This is considered one of Central Europe's finest examples of Late Baroque church architecture.

One of the Apostles from the row of sculptures.

The two gates through the wall
around St. Andrew's Church
feature saintly likenesses from
the 17th and 18th century.

The Romanesque 11th-century Church
of St. Andrew on Grodzka Street. It was
apparently the only Kraków church
to have resisted the Tartar incursions of 1241.

This main portal made from black marble in 1693 adorns
the elevation of the Convent of the Poor Clare Order
adjacent to St. Andrew's Church.

The view from the Wawel Hill of the Baroque dome of St. Peter and Paul's Church and the Romanesque St. Andrew's Church.

The view of the Royal residence on the Wawel Hill from the small defile at the foot of the modest St. Giles's Church.

Dressed in their historical uniforms, members of Krakow's Brotherhood of the Cockerel process with a silver cockerel to the Na Skałce Church.

*The Wawel Hill is beautifully situated above the Vistula, and it was here that great buildings
were erected: the Gothic-Renaissance style Royal Castle, the Gothic Cathedral and defensive walls and towers.*

A coat of arms on the wall of the Vasa Chapel.

The Wawel Cathedral with the Clocktower and Zymuntowska (Sigismund) Tower, the latter holding Poland's largest bell – also called "Sigismund", which was cast in 1520. This weighs some 11 tonnes and has a diameter in excess of two metres.

The Monument to Tadeusz Kościuszko on the Wawel Hill was unveiled in 1921, having been cast from a model by Lvov-based sculptor Leonard Marconi.

The Royal Cathedral on the Wawel Hill is the most important place of worship linked with the history, not only of Kraków, but also of the whole nation. This has been a place of coronations, royal weddings and funerals, as well as of great celebrations offering thanks for Polish successes.

The bones of a mammoth hang by the main entrance to the Wawel Cathedral.

A Gothic-style bas-relief by the Cathedral's main entrance.

The Cathedral door with multiple versions of the monogram K, for King Kazimierz the Great, in whose reign this place of worship was finally completed.

The Baroque-style Chapel of the Vasa family and the Renaissance Zygmuntowska Chapel, whose dome was covered with gold given by Queen Anna Jagiellonka in the years 1591-1592.

The brick wall before the entrance incorporates stone details from the Cathedral that were removed during the renovation work of 1895-1910.

The southern gateway in the wall surrounding the Wawel Cathedral: it was this way that the Kings passed en route for their coronation ceremonies.

A statue by the dome of the Vasa Chapel.

The stained-glass window
by Włodzimierz Tetmajer
in the Cathedral.

The Royal Cathedral on the Wawel Hill
was funded by King Władysław
the Short (reigning 1306-1333)
as a sanctuary for the relics
of St. Stanisław revered by Poles.
It takes the form of a basilica with
nave, two aisles, a transept
and ambulatory.

One of the four 17th-century
tapestries hanging in the nave
of the Wawel Cathedral.
It presents scenes from
the life and times of the
patriarch James, and originated
from the workshop of Jacob
van Zeunen of Brussels.

The Confession of St. Stanisław,
with the relics in a coffin of engraved
sheet silver, is to be found beneath
the dome of the nave.

The symbolic sarcophagus of King Władysław of Varna (reigning 1434-1444).

The Tomb of King Władysław Jagiełło. Renaissance Canopy founded by King Zygmunt the Old.

The Neo-Gothic tomb of Queen Jadwiga (reigning 1384-1399) is fashioned from white marble.

The Cathedral's Holy Cross Chapel dates back to the mid 15th century.

The sarcophagus of King
Kazimierz the Great.

Dating back to 1502-1505,
the tombstone of King Jan Olbracht
is the earliest Renaissance work in Poland.

The tomb of royal couple
Michał Korybut Wiśniowiecki and Eleonora
forms a combined composition with
the adjacent tomb of King Jan III Sobieski.

Built of stone and red marble,
the Zygmuntowska (Sigismund)
Chapel is a true jewel of Renaissance
art serving as mausoleum for the last
Kings of the Jagiellonian Dynasty.

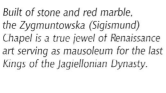

The two early 17th-century bronze
gates leading from the chancel
to the ambulatory are the work
of Maciej Świątek.

The Late Baroque (18th-century)
wall tomb of King Jan III Sobieski
and Queen Maria Kazimiera.

The Royal Castle on the Wawel Hill as seen from the east with its characteristic "hen's foot" corner. The Castle holds a collection of arrases (wall-hangings), national memorabilia, paintings, textiles and antique furniture.

The Sandormierz Tower, one of three defensive towers on the Wawel Hill.

The view of the Wawel Cathedral and castle from the Złodziejski (Thief's) Tower side.

Old cannons in the Wawel courtyard.

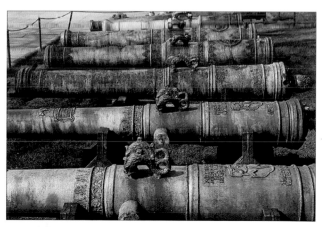

A detail of the vaulting in the gateway to the Royal Castle.

The huge arcaded courtyard of the Wawel Castle.

Steps leading to the first floor with slender columns strengthened at mid height.

The Wawel Armoury: a display
of Mediaeval arms and armour.

The southern elevation of the castle courtyard
is decorated by a painted frieze to be found
on the second story of the cloisters.

In the Crown Treasury, the sword
and hat of King Jan III Sobieski.

The Castle Chapel is from c. 1602. Its vaults feature stucco-work decoration, augmented by painted ceilings from the brush of Józef Pankiewicz dating back to the years 1930-1932.

The Tournament Hall with its Renaissance Italian furniture: a Siena table. Florentine sideboards, Persian carpet from the 19th century and 18th century furnace.

The coffered ceiling of the Chamber of Deputies, otherwise known as the "Under the Heads" Hall. All the heads filling the panels were designed in the early 19th century.

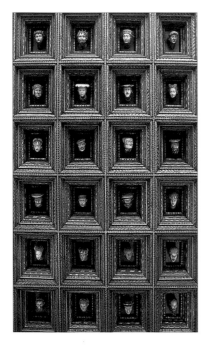

The Zygmunt Tapestry, the largest in the series "Building the Tower of Babel", features the figure of Nimrod. It is to be found in the "Under the Zodiac" Room.

The "Battle of Orsha 1515" Room in the northern wing of the Castle. The painting on another wall depicts "The Battle of Lepanto" by Tomasz Dolabella, court artist to King Zygmunt III.

The "Under the Zodiac" Room was decorated in 1929 with a wall frieze presenting the signs of the zodiac.
It also features King Zygmunt wall-hangings of the series "The Building of the Tower of Babel".

The view of the buildings on Wawel Hill from the east. To be seen from left to right are the Zegarowa (Clock), Senatorska (Senators') and Jordanka Towers. Visible on the right is the top part of the Bernardine church.

The outline foundations of the former Gothic construction on the Wawel Hill, with the Sandomierz Tower in the background.

The Wawel Dragon – a sculpture before the entrance to the Dragon Cave.

Part of the Wawel's defensive walls.

The Pauline Church on the Rock stands on a promontory beyond the Wawel Hill;
its Crypt of Honour holds the earthly remains of many outstanding Poles.

Each year, St. Stanisław's Day (May 8th) brings out thousands of worshippers for the procession leading down from the Wawel Hill to the Na Skałce church (Church on the Cliff).

The May procession is led by the Primate of Poland, currently Cardinal Józef Glemp – seen here among other heads of the Church.

*The Church of Sts. Catherine and Margaret
is part of the Augustinian monastery complex.*

The Gothic-style Church of Sts. Catherine and Margaret, and the old belltower.

The interior of the Church of Sts. Catherine and Margaret features a monumental high altar surviving from 1634.

The neo-Gothic stalls in the church presbytery have painted representations of the saints in their recesses.

The Late Baroque Church of the Brothers of the Order of St. John (formerly of the Trinitarians).

A tenement house by Wolnica Square.

The attic of Kazimierz Town Hall is decorated by bas-relief forms that are work of Wacław Taranczewski from the beginning of the 20th century.

The former Kazimierz Town Hall on Wolnica Square is today the seat of the Ethnographic Museum. This 15th century building features a characteristic tower added a century later.

Wolnica Square and the Corpus Christi Church. Work on the Church began c. 1340 with funding from King Kazimierz the Great. It continued until the beginning of the 15th century. The huge high altar (built 1634-1637) includes a painting of "The Nativity" by Tomasz Dolabella.

The interior of the Corpus Christi Church.

The High Synagogue, dating back to the late 16th century, is now home to the workshops of the Conservator of Monuments.

This Monument on Szeroka Street honours the memory of Jews murdered during the Second World War.

This Baroque-style Jewish place of worship is the Izaak or Ajzyk Synagogue. It is now home to the Centre for Jewish Education.

The Stara Bożnica (Old Synagogue) is indeed Poland's oldest. Today it serves as the museum of Kraków Jewry.

A detail from the palings surrounding the Old Synagogue.

Part of the Szeroka Street façade of the Old Synagogue.

In the eastern wall of the Remuh Synagogue is the Aron ha Kodesh with its deep rectangular recess to hold the scrolls of the Tora.

The entrance door to the almemar in the Remuh Synagogue.

The exit from the Remuh Synagogue and Cemetery.

The Remuh Synagogue is a house of prayer for Orthodox Jews. It was founded around 1553, by Israel Isserles, father of Remuh's Rabbi Moses Isserles.

The Wailing Wall of the Remuh Cemetery recalls the tragic fate met by Kraków Jewry during World War II.

*To this day, the Jewish Cemetery remains a place
of burial for those of the Jewish faith.*

Szeroka Street (the pre-War Szeroki Square)
is surrounded by the largest aggregation
of objects of Jewish architectural heritage.

The nooks and crannies
of old Kazimierz retain their unique atmosphere.

The "Alef" Restaurant offers a hint of the pre-War atmosphere of Kazimierz, allowing one to order traditional Jewish dishes and listen to concerts of klezmer music.

The way into the "Ariel" Restaurant at 18 Szeroka Street.

The Restaurant in Kazimierz.

| Cover photo: | St. Mary's Church. |
| Photo on title page: | A panorama of the Main Market Square with the Cloth Hall, the Gothic-style Mariacki (St. Mary's) Church and Church of St. Adalbert. |

Photos:	CHRISTIAN PARMA
Text:	ELŻBIETA MICHALSKA
Translation:	JAMES RICHARDS
Map:	MARIUSZ SZELEREWICZ
Layout:	BOGNA PARMA, EWA KRELISZYN
Printing:	DRUK INTRO S.A.
Publishers:	Wydawnictwo PARMA PRESS Sp. z o.o. 05 270 Marki, ul. Piłsudskiego 189 b +48 22/ 781 16 48, 781 16 49, 781 12 31 e-mail: wydawnictwo@parmapress.com.pl http://www.parmapress.com.pl

ISBN 83-7419-025-6